# The Second Symphony

# I Got Beaten
# by the First Dagger of Desire

## Nadia Abu Shama

## Dr. M.E. Fayad

# Brilliant Stars in the Sky of Literature and Writing

My sophisticated erudite student, Nadia Abu Shama, is of Algerian origin. She is a distinguished writer, an eloquent first-class person, and a talented writer. In a fantasy world other than that one you live, you are under a spell with her charming words, dancing with her messages. She is able to stir up all the sorrows confined in your deep recesses, so as to perceive the universe with the eyes of purity, serenity, and childish ecstasy.

She was born and brought up in the Babur Mountains - the city hanging at the foot of a large mountain with a geographical and historical heritage and home to revolutionaries during the French occupation, where great revolutions and battles took place. This region of enchanting and rare beauty was very isolated and remote from the capital city , just like a pearl or an expensive diamond concealed from all the world's eyes.

Collaborating with Dr. Fayad, she has written thoughts, in the form of letters, and more than forty books, "Universal Symphonies." Examples of her masterpieces are: "The Novel of Al-Taffar" , "The Nude Body," "The Legend," "Dancing on Water," "The Ram Dancer," "The Gazelle of Al-Bawadi," "The Prisoner of the Past," and "The Rape of a Woman."

0000000

Dr. Mohamed Fayad, an American of Egyptian origin, spent more than forty years, dedicating his life to the niche of knowledge, and spending the best days of his life in fruitful scientific research. Then generations, graduated under his supervision and sponsorship, believed in the value of science and learning, which contributed indirectly to the renaissance and development of America and other countries of the world through multiple expeditionary trips to spread knowledge around the globe.

Dr. Mohamed Fayad contributed positively and globally to raising the status of human civilization in the world and participated in composing the "Cosmic Symphonies". Among his scientific, literary and reform works, he published ten scientific and permanent books and more than 500 scientific articles in the most famous scientific journals and conferences. And add to this, his striving to spread his innovations in the "Engineering of Unified Words", "the Unified and Stable Linguistic Engineering", "the Engineering of the Unified Field", and "the Art of Abstraction" . This is all with God's help.

# Dedication

To all the homelands that were abandoned by their migratory birds, where the beautiful love stories had come to an end.

Nothing was left with us but feelings that were retrieved to surprise us, to kill us, and to tear our loving souls apart.

To that wounded heart that consoles and comforts itself with the messages of his old lover.

To that heart whose memories devour it, just like an unbearable flood.

To that heart which has been torn apart by estrangement, wandering, and searching for the face of his beloved..... .

*Nadia Abu Shama*

Why, on every object, must I see your face?
As if you are, on earth, all the human race,
As if you are a long path, without an end.
I was made for this journey. You must comprehend.
If I were from you to you running away, you see.
Lord, where's the escape!?" So, please, tell me.
*Farouk Jewaida*

**Dr. M.E. Fayad**

# Table Of Contents

# 1

# I Departed...

The words and letters would blame me because I had not said them to you before you left.

I did not let your ears hear their sweet rhythmic tone as they waved swaying near them.

If so, they would flirt with you and keep you close to me.

If so, they would make your heart filled with bliss and gaiety.

If so, your feelings would fly like soap bubbles that children play with.

All the language dictionaries moved like armies to kill what was left of me.

They would penetrate my emaciated body in the presence of your absence.

As if time, with its hours, moments, minutes, seconds, nights, days, months and years, had plotted to tear my longings for you with a knife, and squeeze me so as to be close to you.

I wish I did not love you, or even I had the ability to forget you.

I wanted to forget you the first minute you left me.

However, I was defeated by the first dagger of longing, that was placed on the neck of the eagerness and desire to see you.

This was not loyalty nor sincerity from me, but it was my weakness and defeat in front of your presence within me.

As you were swimming with the oars of existence within me, you moved the wakeful pain and the ache, which was waiting in my blood.

And you would storm deep inside me like a winter blizzard.

I would search for your scent everywhere, in all corners, to warm myself, to hide myself behind your perfume even for a second.

Your departure was out of my hand, but I am now steadfast in your absence, anticipating a time when love will be regarded as an endless relationship between people. I am waiting for a time when yearning will be regarded as a result of eternal love; for a time when warm emotions are recognized as a source of life and survival alike.

After your departure, I became like a stranger, wandering the streets of life, asking everyone on the roads about the date of your return; and begging time for the moment of your arrival, just like that of a crescent moon.

I am not guilty of my attachment to you, and I am not the reason for your departure.

But I have to pay an exorbitant bill out of my life and my days, the items of which are all pain, torment and longings that boil like strong fires extending their flames up to space.

Where did that bright face disappear, and that smile that used to encircle me, like the chains of an executioner, and tie the vein of my sad heart?

Where is that mess that you used to create with your hustle and continuous laughter; with your indiscretions that I always referred to be that of youth?

I convince myself that one day I will be able to bridle them, and control the mighty frenzied stallion inside you.

I wonder, was I laughing at myself at the time?

I feel sad without you and without your chaos that I have often complained about.

At that time, I criticized all your behaviors.

I was dying with all methods of death when your voice would echo far from my earshot.

How much I was entertained by those incidents that would always take place, when you would trip over and things would fall from your hands!

I recalled the loud music that you would always stretch out your hand to turn up, but I constantly stretch out my hand to turn down.

All places, roads and gardens are miserable in your absence.

I no longer hear your sarcastic comments, with the spontaneity of a child, on all the things around us.

Do you really have to keep punishing me like my father, and never forgive the sin of my love?

You punished me the day I loved you so violently, excessively and jealously.

I wanted to curb the lively life that spreads within you like green fields.

You punished me when you had left me.

So, waiting for you would break me with a harsh hammer with its constant blows as if breaking hard rocks.

Just tell me about your destination and I will come to you like lightning.

After that I will be like restive horses, chaos and clamor.

I will be like the wine of life as well as the drunk one who can no longer get drunk with your love more than before.

I can no longer carry my body that sways all the time.

My soul, within my body, always moans because of your absence all the time. The music, I used to hear with you, screamed in my ears.

All the whispers of yours would slaughter me; all the tenderness, I used to have, would hurt me like thorns and palm-reeds.

After your inevitable departure, I never returned. Everything within me has changed except my heart, which is still your abode and your refuge.

Your love alone is my ship that I ride, like a purebred horse, wanting it to sail and never stop.

How much I have changed after you: my existence and all the usual things within me. No longer did I know how to distinguish the spectrum of colors, one from another.

Even the theater seats had become sad and miserable when I would try to sit on them, I would laugh at all the chapters of the comedy play, while my heart was absent-minded and depressed.

It would wail like a bereaved woman whose husband and children had passed away.

# 2

# But we have a date together...

Oh desert: how much you drowned, overwhelmed and swallowed nations with your powerful whirlwinds!

How much your eerie silence killed, and your interior was filled with lots and lots!

However, you did not reveal to anyone your stories, or your mighty power.

Everyone kept heading towards you, not caring about your mystery and the inevitable death within you.

I loved your sands and your sun, and your palm oasis and all your dates.

I loved your rare lakes, and your long nights.

I used to enjoy your stillness and flirt with your silence.

I adored you as you were the home of my beloved.

My beloved, who followed her imagination to appear in a Bedouin look with her silver earrings colored in red, green, yellow and blue.

She would wrap her graceful stature with an embroidered cloth around her slender body.

She wipes it with the color of the indigo that shines when it collides with the sun's rays.

The anklets were superimposed on top of each other, and her bracelets clung to her wrist up to her elbow.

All her silver jewelry would make a sound that was perhaps the only sound that would tickle your stillness and awe.

Only her jewelry was challenging you and everything inside you.

My Beauty! Being alone, she never feared or trembled at the advent of your whirlwinds and peril.

She used to go fetch water with her pottery pot decorated with Berber drawings and symbols whose meanings I do not comprehend.

She used to look at her face on the surface of the lake, with her braid dangling each one from one side, while her smile adorned everything there.

You, desert, were frightening and terrifying despite your silence and your divine splendor.

My beloved was running and strutting in her gait; her steps were faltering when she would approach my tent.

At that time, I was just wandering just like a tourist, or an artist who would play the guitar at night, and paint during the day.

Then, I turned into a citizen who would defy your doom and ride your whirlwinds like the waves of the sea.

I would cover my face with a piece of blue cloth and follow your shadow and the smell of your breath.

I did not see you .. I did not know you till I formed you in my imagination.

The books on the shelves of the American University library tell about a desert that resembles a snake in its sting, a peacock in its beauty, and the night in its stillness.

I played lots of music, and her voice became more beautiful and sweeter when you folded her in your arms and embraced her with your heart.

You drew a solfège[1] for her with the pencils of your eyelashes.

I turned the silence of the desert into praises, hymns, and nocturnal monologues.

I turned our groans into a love ecstasy from which I never wake up.

I sipped love, longing, and eagerness instead of date syrup.

I remember the moment she glowed inside me, but I can't remember when she was extinguished.

The silent desert was surrounded by my melodies, joy, and longing.

She complained about following your footsteps and hearing the sounds of your anklets and bracelets, disturbing her security and silence, and clouding her night with my chanting and playing for long hours.

The cups of tea, prepared on hot coals, were filled, then empty, then refilled; and spinning on those who were present.

_______________________________

[1] Solfège or solfeggio is the study of singing and musicianship using solmization syllables.

Their circle grew larger and larger, as my melodies and the sound of my guitar were intoxicating them.

The wrath of the desert crept up and swallowed you up in a blink of an eye. The pure golden grains of sand enveloped you just like a pure bride's dress.

It offered you to death to marry, offered you as a sacrifice to its arrogance and tyranny.

Our eyes followed the hands of the sand as they were holding you like thorny branches of a mulberry tree.

In the meantime, you shouted and flopped, as your eyes were staring at me.

I tried to run towards you, but a human hand grabbed me and pulled me by a wall of palm fronds, where we hid.

How strong you are, O desert, with your sand armies!

Yet, I have no response, while your love, in my heart, is steady like mountains and pegs!

The guitar in my hand has turned into a sad flute.

I play your sorrowful lyrics every day.

I cry for you in a miserable melody and a murderous longing.

It was not only "Hizia"[2] who died at the desert gate, and her lover sang for her and made her a long poem that has lived with us up to now.

---

[22] Hizia and Said is an Algerian Bedouin love story that took place in the second half of the nineteenth century in the town of Biskra, in southeastern Algeria. It is similar to the stories of the virgins in the ancient Arab heritage, or the story of Romeo and Juliet, and others.

Here you have everything within me.

You take me to times I do not know, play melodies that I am not used to, and laugh in the home of sorrows, and grieve in places of joy and pleasure.

Your flowery face is formed every night in the stillness of the universe and takes me to the grains of sand that I want to dispose of, one by one.

Together with the sand dunes, I watch how the wind shifts them from one place to another.

I find my longing bound to me, and my eagerness to meet you suffocates me like the arms of sand that encircled you that night.

How hard you are, O flute, which cries out my pain every night, and tell about my anguish in a low voice! But, its blade is sharp, as it is slaughtering me from head to toe.

# 3

# It is nothing more than a disagreement....

You are move within my being like a cigarette, which your fingers are addicted to hold, rotate, and inhale, or like the nectar of oxygen and distilled perfume nitrates.

You are travelling in your depths like a seagull, so are all your senses travelling as well.

You are formed into another human being.

You sing to yourself your favorite song.

How much would I love to bicker with you?

Then I would make up all the excuses for you.

I would hurry to throw myself on you like a raging, rough wave falling on the seashore and vanishing like foam.

I would turn your turbid mood with my words fleeing from me to you.

I would embrace you like a small child, tired of searching for a new adventure and mischief in an innovative manner.

It is not strange that I was addicted to you and would fly into you.

All human beings are addicted to various things, and this addiction differs in some way or another.

I would not blame myself for that, whether it was revealed to me or concealed from me.

For in your gaze there are complete dictionaries of poetry.

There are also words, arranged and seductive, like bottles of wine and their glasses with dim light.

Some of them are suspended, whereas others are arranged in a geometric way.

Likewise, tables are decorated with candles whose dim luster gives endless calm and romance to the place.

Everyone was sitting sipping their drink as ecstasy would elevate them.

For in every addiction there is ecstasy, departure and deep faith that we are not able to describe?

Inside every person there is a place for wine, from which they drink to reach their desired ecstasy.

And with their addiction they reach the climax of faith.

Faith is within every human being.

Every one of us shapes it in the mold of their love, feelings and pains.

Some of us travel in the kingdom of God, giving praises, love and thanksgiving to their God.

Another one of us loves their library, and what it possesses of old paper books, where they sail through their seas and drown in prayers with letters and authors for long hours.

Others are happy to be indulged in their works that they master.

Others are happy and sophisticated with their families and children.

And many others get lost in their hobbies that they cling to madly.

So, no one is to blame me if I cling to you to the point of madness.

And if I would enter the sanctity of the universe and be attracted to a history that I could not realize.

You brought me to places whose addresses or laws I would not know.

They are similar to kingdoms, cities, or countries, but their laws are different from the ones which humans make for themselves.

I need so much to throw myself in your arms and sleep like a little girl and be free from you and for you.

I need so much to be like that kitten which curls itself when it feels afraid or lost, turning around when it is lonely and strange.

I want to hang all my cities in your handsome countenance, and build many bridges between my heart and your blood flow, so that they lead me to your righteous paradise, or bring me back to you.

Being away from you makes me torn and devastated in the first moments of longing, makes me weaker in the first beats of my heart.

Haven't I told you that my love is like addiction to things, the one, who is addicted, is always broken and weak.

My heart softens whenever your fantasies cross my memories, whenever nostalgia pulls me to the cities of your eyes.

I feel crying, screaming and wailing like martyrs' widows.

Your love slaughters me like a lamb that is the sacrifice of Eid[3].

You capture me in this vast world, but I am like a prisoner sentenced to death, whose legs are shackled with iron chains.

How could you reach my heart and build all these storeys for yourself?

You penetrated within me more than my pains, groans, and hopes. You ascended within me like the birds' melody.

How could you the conquer the tyranny of my pride and curb my reckless steps?

You tied me so tightly that neither the knots nor the cords would break.

______________________________

[3] The Feast of Sacrifice which is celebrated by Muslims all over the world as a major holiday for a period of three to four days.

# 4

# And much was said that I didn't love you...

Some people whisper in her ears and say:" He does not love you and if he loves you, he will not be yours, because no laws bind him to the lands of love and the orchards of passion.

He is reckless and loves wandering.

So, he will be just a passer-by in your life.

All the words you used to hear from him were mere illusion and poetry from the weaving of his charming tongue, because he was trying to sweep off your feet and numb all your glowing senses to follow him like a raging mare running away, dancing with her seductive body, all proud of her strength, energy and activity."

He derives strength from all that is within you to scatter into existence like hailstones and white pieces of snow.

Be sure, O kitten, who is always fleeing to the balls of his eyes, that he eludes and deludes you with love in order to get you into his chaotic cities, and draw within you the days fleeing from him.

He tries to turn the sparkle of bliss and pleasure in your eyes into tears that sparkle like pearls.

He tries to steal the pink color from your cheeks and retain the bright sparkle of your eyes, because every lover keeps swaying between joy and sadness, in which hope and gloom are repeated.

For sure, in love the fight and flight are just like battles.

He loves your falling in his hands like an olive branch hanging over every house gate, to be proud of his might and win the bet.

Whoever tells you that, in this age, there is a heart that beats, or a soul that gets lost in passion, collect all their poems given to you and throw them in the trash.

Make sure that all of our generation does not appreciate feelings and does nothing but messing around in his field.

Were you seduced by his words and influenced by his poetry and sweet music?

We are a group of humans whose hearts are lazy, broken and idle.

Give him all his poems back, and change your phone numbers and social sites as well.

Give him a wrong address, a fake phone number, and dates that will never be.

This is our way of love.

This is what's going on in our world now.

So, how are you so naive?

And how can you be craftily eluded like that?

How can you read between the lines?

Do search the record of his life, you will find many examples of slain women like you, who fell in love with him.

He deluded them all as he claimed himself to be their only lover.

Then he left them all behind his back the same way he left the years of his age, not caring about their screams or pains.

He was not moved by their cries or moans.

He left her as a martyr of an unknown battle.

How did you believe him, or believe his outdated poems, and his eloquent words embroidered with grammar and morphology, surpassing all the classic poetic meters?

Say that you only liked his poetic singing, and your heart was not shaken by this passion.

So, if you read his poems anymore, know that it was the only way that would entertain him.

He loved messing with words and dancing with them.

He tickled the depths of the sleeping youth away from the noise of life.

Away from hustle and bustle, indecency and falsehood.

# 5

# A Lover's Heartbeat

The airports of many countries receive me, with their glass airport lounges full of noise, smart flight attendants and travelers' eyes in which nostalgia, dream and pain mix.

My eyes have only your image.

I ran towards it as I was breathing life in from the depths of the universe.

As I was wandering in several gardens to taste the beauty of its flowers, roses, and the splendor of spring as well.

You were the conqueror without armies, and the one chained me without chains.

How much I loved to travel from your eyes to another land.

Otherwise, you would travel with me on an eternal journey to the whole world.

You would hide under my wings whilst you were as close to me as my heartbeat.

I used to sip my cup of coffee as I was lost at the gateway to your temple.

What prayers and hymns would I say to you?

All my travels no longer concern me after they were large parts extracted from my dreams.

Here I am going and coming with my passport and ticket in one hand, and my bag in the other.

But my mind and everything within me is leaving to where you are.

Leaving to where the sun rises and the four seasons begin.

Leaving to the land where it rains wherever you live.

Leaving to where spring blooms and the birds twitter, to where the nightingales sing and the butterflies fly.

Your images are looming wherever my sight falls.

Then I was surrounded by my memories, my nostalgia, my little village with all its narrow streets and alleys.

I was encircled by the mulberry trees and their thorny branches that mark every orchard.

I was enfolded by those houses that are close to one another, with their similar doors, windows, small balconies, and house yards.

We all were sipping our coffee and tea and eating the most delicious cakes at a table, large enough for all of us.

At that time, I would secretly dance with your eyelashes in every lonely corner of the night.

I would exchange its darkness with light pink and rosy colors.

I used to make myself beautiful rainbow-like dreams and make up a lot of dialogues and stories, just like episodes of current TV series.

Can you remember how many letters of love I wrote to you?

How many poems did I compose for you?

However, I tore them all up after that.

I did so, because every time I would discover that all the words I had said and all my poetry I had composed were not apt to what my heart would like to say to you, nor to what you would expect to hear.

Now I come to know that the true language of the heart is only silence, and that the true words of love are those that we never say, those that remain concealed in our depths.

Your eyes were the sea where I would love drowning.

I loved the nights and all the sorrows that suddenly arose in your eyeballs.

Every time I was unable to interpret their meaning, as I once believed that the eyes are the true tell-tale of the lover's depths of heart.

But not a single time was I able to understand their ambiguity, sadness or suffering.

Am I then a failure at reading eyes?

Or is what goes on inside me is more overwhelming than just interpreting my distracted eyes into you?

Or with your mystery, sadness, and strong ambition, you were a barrier, with a new occupier, to my distressed heart.

Such a small village with its simple joys, weddings, summers, people, and your being there, was like a hijacked piece of the universe, different to this one.

As if my imagination, wandering about you, made me aspire to be another universe other than this one, to which we could travel.

So, I could escape alone with my breaths, dreams, hopes, and testimonies in order to give you the right to take refuge in a planet other than this one.

So, I could make a history about you other than ours.

So, I could sail you away from these seas, and lead you as a princess to countries that humans have never known.

You were greater in knowledge than mathematics, physics, and electronic industries that I went through in my laboratory.

You were more melodious than all poetry and loftier than all love. You were more sophisticated than all literature.

I never know how my dreams about you swept me away to places more spacious than this universe?

I was waging wars against armies that I had never seen before in my life.

What kind of female are you who confined my soul to paper and pen?

You limited my existence to strange dreams and endless ambition.

From you I have learned about travels.

At that time, I realized that it was my destiny because I made it my biggest dream.

Nevertheless, I never thought that I would travel alone and keep waiting for your name to be announced in the loudspeaker at the airport while the names of people are called for every flight.

So, it was my destiny to travel when you were near me. I used to travel everywhere with you through my dreams.

And now, here I am traveling everywhere and trying to bring you with me, whether you were a dream or a reality!

You made a dream, an aspiration and a homeland, all this for me.

For me you made a history and adorned the walls of my office with many testimonies.

You colored my heart with sparkling and brilliant diamonds, rare to be found in any existing place.

You have become the obsession that haunts me everywhere, just as my dreams used to chase me and compel me to be away from you against my will.

You never were yourself, and I never made you a homeland, history or an existence.

Neither did you accompany me on all my travels nor did I recover from you and your bleeding love.

Every day I am to be tested, subjugated, and flogged.

They stamp my passport with "Relentless Lover".

They tattoo my right arm with the initials of your name.

However, they never mention to me the time of our date, nor even our destination.

Tell me by God, the Creator of the universe, what are you seeking from me after all this? What do you intend to do to me?

In your presence I am a lost little child whose tongue stutters.

All my letters are lost.

I forget the date of my birth.

I do not know my homeland or the reason for my existence.

For my birth is determined by your dating with me.

My years of lifetime are calculated from the date you received my heart.

Your eyes are my only abode.

# 6

# Live in love as long as you like

The world will sweep you away in all directions.

Your heart will continue to drag you only in one direction,

Like a compass that does not lose its function.

Love will continue to sing with all your spiritual powers.

It will glow and lighten you with all its fires.

It will give you a soul that dances in the Universe corners.

It will make you transcend the futility of time.

You will search for nothing as all that people have searched for is yours.

You contain it all, and love alone envelops you as does the air with the universe.

You need not to prove to anyone that you are immersed in a world different from the ordinary world.

For you alone are tasting ecstasy, worshipping reverently in its temples.

You light candles for her every morning and every evening, and you never end.

You whisper in her ears poems that no one else can comprehend.

You will tell her a lot about what your tender heart does contain.

But every time she tells you that you said nothing about her again.

I only see words in your eyes.

Yet, you swear by the greatness of the Most Merciful God that you recite many new poems to her every day.

She assures you that she did not hear any poetry from you.

But she always replies that she knows well your heart.

It calls out to her like a worshiper, shunning all women.

You write poems for her like a rebellious poet who was afflicted by madness when he drowned in her eyes.

You are alone with her and with your pink dreams.

So, you travel from your soul to embrace her soul.

You smell her scent and put on her perfume.

For her sake you will change the laws of the universe.

Since she is within you like a sea wave eroding the sands of the beach.

You will resolve not to leave her, to always love her, as you cannot live without an eager heart.

You cannot live without her presence within you as your artery and your forming elements.

It is said that you will leave her or that she has left you.

However, you assert that she lives within you.

How can a worshiper quit the pleasure of worshipping?!

How can a mystic be betrayed by his senses?!

For him death means nothing, just as life without the scent of her hair is not a true life. It doesn't count.

# 7

# Because poetry is in my blood...

Look! you surprised me by entering the kingdom of my life.

You spread all your armies in the corners of my soul.

You stayed in my fleet, and shifted the compass of my history.

As a result, I surprised my audience when I recited the first poem of this year.

It was in the first season of the year.

It was about the map of the homeland and all its borders.

All the borders of the homeland turned into a female, which is YOU.

what does Home mean if it is devoid of you or if you do not contain it?

The audience was amazed when they saw plenty of bleeding, deportation, killing, displacement and destruction.

The homeland then turned into a beautiful woman's face whose reunion we aspire.

We dream of her splendor as we are longing constantly for her.

We crave her warm embrace, whilst her arms holding us and bandaging our wounds.

Bullets, cannons and missiles turned into words as I used to say.

However, I was writing about a love that tore me apart,

About a love that engraved me on a piece of gold and stuck me in your bosom and heart.

About a woman who conquers me without mercy.

About broken letters like ice melting on coming near the sun.

Then they commit suicide in its light, and soon they are done.

I was writing about you...Oh, my beloved One!

About the armies of your eyes that invaded the land of my heart.

And they turned me into a citizen who loves death by the bullets of your soul.

I turned over the pages of all the books and dictionaries looking for the words that are suitable for you.

I read all the classical poetry searching its verses about the appropriate vocabulary, with its synonyms, to write you a poem that surpasses all the poets' verses.

I went to stay up watching the leaves, the moon and the night.

And how long without you was that dreary night.

I wrote a lot and tore a lot as all the letters are not worthy of your beauty.

Not worthy of your description as they proved their futility.

You were like an earthquake rocking my place.

I never knew its strength, as it was greater than any earthquake afflicted all the human race.

All my audience were baffled by my words, and that was the case.

I went on completing the rest of the words as they come out of my throat crawling towards eternity.

They were surmounted by innate shyness and defiance.

They were singing like the notes of a flute that descend from the highest peak of the mountain to the bottom of the valley.

They were like a series of sounds that start high and end low like all endings.

All the eyes that watch me are devoid of your crystal luster that radiates like jewels.

I cannot hear all the cheers because they suddenly turn into your melodious whispers that I have long waited to hear from you.

I will write about you now, later and for ever.

I will transform all my history to dedicate you my all poems.

I will compete with everyone who sang and wrote poetry in ink.

I will scatter you in history like grains of wheat, like green shoots.

I will leave you behind like the leaves of a sunflower.

For you alone are my spring and my paradise, and the succession of my days.

I will bring you to my eyes like the sunlight, creeping to the end of the day.

And I will make you in the outskirts of my heart as my robe that warms me in the middle of frost and winter.

I  need neither tickets from you nor the addresses of your favorite places.

I do not need your bumpy roads that you always take to escape from the hell of my longings.

For I am your shadow that does not leave your company.

The audience clapped long for me and stood up as well.

I was like a bird that felt neither space nor time as I was really flying in my pink dreams.

I was like embracing the highest skies.

I paid no attention to all the noise and cheering in the hall, nor to the flashes of the cameras.

Only you were the one reciting my poems and addressing all my audience.

Take my papers and pens away from me.

Hasten to free me from the cheering of the masses and let me get down from the stage of the auditorium.

Words are falling like winter rains.

You blow like the winds and travel with me among the stars and planets.

Do I live in the earth, Mars, Saturn, the moon, or another planet?

Do not say I am a poet or a writer, just write in my tombstone: "A lover of the first class", who whenever your passion hurts him, he plants a jasmine tree and Cestrum nocturnum.

Whenever your passion hurts him, he goes crying like children.

Whenever he gets nostalgic, he makes a kite and writes many phrases on it, hanging it in a thread and lifting it to the sky, and thinking that it will reach you.

Whenever longing squeezes me, I go write letters to you at the time of non-messages and send them to you in a glass bottle.

I throw them to the waves of the sea, thinking that you will pick them up when you are at the edge of the beach, and saying your seclusion and night-long prayers.

Humans! How cruel it is for a female to occupy you and turn you into her followers, even though you have never seen her!

You call it the homeland at times.

You call it alienation at other times.

You call it the dreamy land, and name it: "the mistress of the world and the collections of poetry."

# 8

## My adoration to you is much further than the usual meaning of love

My craving for writing and spinning with twisted letters has already increased.

I used to generate words effortlessly at the morning sunshine that almost would cover my little town.

In the meantime, the cold breeze would brush and encircle our bodies.

How beautiful this weather is in August, especially its last days.

There are many regions in the world on fire, under the scorching sun.

As scorching as many people who themselves are flaming and burning.

How so much I adore you, my love.

For every day you fascinate me more.

I love the strength of your personality and your constant care.

I love in you the strong Pharaoh who is full of arrogance, fathers' affection, and the lover 's madness.

I love all about you: your elegant speech, your continuous ambition, your organization of things to the point of boredom, your love and passion for life and science.

I love your innate vulnerability, and your feelings burning in a terrible silence.

I love everything about you.

Furthermore, I adore you beyond the usual meaning of love.

I crave you more than I crave all things.

My craving is above.

I don't know why women are always moody.

They always go on a journey of ebbs and flows.

Whilst men rush into love to the point of fascination and bewilderment.

Then they get distracted from you to the point of obliviousness.

Once you tell them about what happens to you during the period of their being away from you, they wonder at your words.

Rather, they get angry, wonder, and get disappointed in you.

**9**

# You are unaware how much I died owing to your absence.

You never know how much I died while you were away from me, a day or a half of day?!

You never know how much the waves of longing shook me because of you?

And how much did l hit the rocks of waiting for you?

You never know how much the fire of waiting devoured me?

And how much it devastated all my feelings?

You never know how I spent a day and a half without hearing your voice?

Without reading your letters?

Without contemplating your face and hugging your laughter!

You never know, my love, how I died away from you?

I was adhering to your promise that you would talk to me in the evening.

But time was moving very slowly .. very slowly !

Time was tickling my waiting, every second, and every moment.

It was judging them in the cage of deprivation and torment.

The hours of my waiting for you this evening were much longer.

Much longer than your meeting time for twenty years, or longer.

I was walking with my faltering steps, dragging them with all my might.

So, I would reach my promised meeting with that night.

I carried in my depths many hopes and dreams,

Many joys tangled like a wild grape arbor, near some streams.

In my mind were all the melodies of Umm Kulthum[4] recalled, So, I would repeat them for you.

I knew that you loved her person and adored her melodious voice.

For that evening I wanted to be dressed up in a bright red garment of natural silk.

It would outline my entire body, with an opening above the knee on the left leg, and a bare back.

My gypsy hair was rushing down my shoulder.

That evening I was at my best good-looking outfit.

I, the evening, the melodies of Umm Kulthum, and the gentle breeze were all together waiting for your arrival.

---

[4] 4- Umm Kulthum (31 December 1898 – 3 February 1975) was an Egyptian singer, songwriter, and film actress active from the 1920s to the 1970s. She is regarded as one of the greatest singers in the history of Arab music.

We were waiting for hearing your voice, and seeing your cheerful facial features.

We all waited and waited for a long time.

I heard the sound of time mocking me: the ticking of the clocks hanging on the walls.

I heard this mockery in Umm Kulthum's melodies as well.

I heard strange voices, which I did not focus on, emanating around me.

I was just waiting for the arrival of the dearest and the most gentle lover whose dates are always exact.

I did not and will not doubt that one day.

One day I received a card from you that says:

"I beg your pardon. I am too busy at work. Stop meditating, please"

The card was sad in tone and totally alone.

Neither a single rose, nor even a single picture was attached to it.

It was devoid of all your usual affections.

It was devoid of all warm feelings that would always wrap you, and which you would always send to me.

It was totally bare.

I held myself up and lifted my bright red dress with my hands and ran to where my miserable pens were.

I did not grieve seriously, but... anyway I grieved.

I excused you as you had been so much busy.

You did not even take a rest from long, arduous travel.

I tried not to disturb you, and not to call you.

I tried to let you work.

I tried to curb the sense of frustration about the promised date in that evening.

The longings were greater than me and the evening itself.

The hours of deadly waiting were longer than the period of all my life.

You could certainly allocate me a short time beside the rest of your work program.

This would be the least of your duties, and the simplest of my rights from you.

You only wanted a strong love that would lift you from your place.

You wanted a broad love that would include you anywhere.

A sweeping love that would take you away from all your world.

A sweeping love that would plant steadfastness and persistence in you.

Do not blame the pen when it writes.

It has promised you that it would convey to you all the dreams and feelings with all credibility.

You agreed to share everything with me.

I will only be able to write you my feelings in all details and sincerity.

If only you experience love and its torment!

If only you do and live its rituals!

My love is strong as it has much ecstasy to the point of flying in a distant space.

It also has a torment that begins as soon as you I don't see your lovely face.

As soon as you are far away from me.

As soon as your words never reach me.

As soon as I hear not your voice.

# 10

# The Photo Album

I held the photo album turning your pictures one after one.

I addressed them in a sad tone full of sorrows.

I was forcing my tongue to move with a great effort.

You seemed to be more upset, to be in more pain than me.

I was very afraid of you, and afraid of losing you.

I was afraid that you would grieve like me.

That you would suffer the pain.

That you would be stripped of life and creativity.

That you would suffer the pain that gnawed at your brain.

I feared for you from the deadly storms of love.

From the aridity of your life's well, as well.

You really need strong love that gives you warmth and safety again.

The meaning of determination is not that your body works hard in order to forget your love.

It is also to reach what you aspire to.

For it is always said,: " In order to forget our pains, we must work hard with our bodies non-stop".

For this you have to create a balance with two equal scales.

Oh, my love, how much I worried about you of sadness first, then of pain second, then of hurt and loneliness.

I forgot everything about myself:

I forgot my sorrows, and I knew that there is no sadness comparable to the sadness of my beloved.

I adapted to sorrows and devoured them all the time.

So, I was forced to adapt to them and get used to them.

I adapted to live with pain.

But, my love, I say "No" a thousand times so that pain won't live with you.

I thought a lot of a way to save you from everything that will suddenly surprise you.

I knew then how much I did you wrong.

How selfish I had been when I wasted your time, knowing that you would madly adore me.

I made sure that our love has other ways than these ways that we take as a course for our meeting.

Yet, I cannot be away from you for a single moment and being away from you is torture.

I cannot bear not to hear your tender voice with which I feel warmth and security.

I cannot bear not to think about you for this is impossible.

Not to care about me is something scary and disturbing.

It is like fleeing from a fire to a fire that is much more severe.

I addressed your pictures, as I saw joy shining in your face.

You never know, my love, how much I loved you and how much I breathed your scent spreading in the air.

I lose my words when I try to express that to you.

I find myself in the midst of a strong whirlwind that uproots all the veins of my body.

It is as if it is a volcano that cracks and releases its fuse to collapse.

# 11

# I was watching you all night while you were up

I used to watch you all night while you were awake.

You were writing like a lover, or researching the secrets of science and nature in depth.

You were working among them as if you had never worked before, all this without seeing me.

I was counting the beats of time how fast they were running while I was near you.

And during you sleep, I used to live with you constantly, moment after moment.

I used to sit by your bed to monitor your heartbeat.

I cover you with a beautiful robe, and arrange your cotton pillow.

I contemplate your life and sail there.

I dance with your breath, and reproach your eyelashes that did not contain me.

They could not contain my soul in the midst of pain.

I reproach your eyesight, which was strained by books and papers, without my being with you.

I rebuke the time that made between us homelands, seas, and long times that we could not measure.

However, I find joy that wraps my depths and tells me that you adore me violently and remember me all your time.

The dear beloved is not only the one we always live with, but also the one for whom we carry love in our depths.

As long as we live and in every place, we find this occupies our mind.

As usual you were very quiet in your sleep.

You were like a beautiful, spoiled child.

You were smiling continuously in your sleep.

On your waking up, you would turn your eyes on my angelic face and extend your arms to hold me tightly.

You would invite me to have breakfast with you on the garden table in the house.

You would give me a beautiful white flower.

You would carry your wallet and go quickly to your work, after you put a kiss on my forehead as a token of this beautiful day.

# 12

# The Insomnia of Loneliness

I was happy when the cloud of sadness, burning, longing and pain went away from you.

You were afraid of separation and pain due to my distance from you.

You were afraid of losing me.

You were afraid that you would neither see nor talk to me.

You were fighting your depths and your heart a strong fight.

At that time I knew how much you were fighting and discriminating between a heart that loves me to the point of madness and a mind that rejects me to the point of arrogance?

Did you know how you fought all the things that block and hinder you from your scientific ambition?

And how did you remove, with the help of God Almighty, huge rocks that were placed as barriers in the way of your success?

How did you sacrifice so many things to get to the top?

You did all this to reach the top of the pyramid of success you planned one day.

But this cursed heart did not follow your plans and overwhelmed you this time.

It rebelled against the strict laws of your mind.

I saw sadness once again and also saw the severe strictness surrounding you from every side.

After that, my love, I feared for your rupture, for your struggle, for your self-dispersion and for your successes.

I will never be the reason for all this.

There must be a fair way for everything.

I am the superpower that occupies you. So, definitely it will not destroy you. It will never eliminate ambition from you.

I'm not the one making a mess of you.

I am just like time. like the click of a clock and a heartbeat.

I thought a lot about what we are up to.

There must be an urgent solution that settles and ends all these differences.

My love is being torn apart.

My love is in pain.

My love has a bleeding wound.

Now I have to be smarter and stronger.

I have to be the wisest and most reasonable woman.

My exaggerated attention kills him and increases his distance as well.

My exaggerated interest confuses everything, disperses his thoughts.

There must be a way out to end this serious dispute.

I must free my beloved from these pains and this chaos that has be-
fallen him, and changed a lot in his life.

I am sure that my beloved will be unconquerable and his resolution
will never weaken.

I promised myself that I would help you with all my will, determination and strength to reach your goals, my love.

www.ingramcontent.com/pod-product-compliance
Lightning Source LLC
Chambersburg PA
CBHW060944130726
48001CB00003B/1060